Table of Contents

SCOTT FORESMAN · ADDISON WESLEY

Mathematics

Kindergarten

Home-School Connection

- Family Letters
- Study Buddies

PEARSON

Scott
Foresman

Editorial Offices: Glenview, Illinois • Parsippany, New Jersey • New York, New York

Sales Offices: Parsippany, New Jersey • Duluth, Georgia • Glenview, Illinois
Coppell, Texas • Ontario, California • Mesa, Arizona

Table of Contents

ISBN: 0-328-03816-4

1 2 3 4 5 6 7 8 9 10 V064 09 08 07 06 05 04 03

FAMILY LETTER

CHAPTER 1

Position and Sorting

Dear Family,

In this chapter, your child will learn to describe the position of objects using words like *over, under, on, inside, outside, left, right, top, middle,* and *bottom.* Your child will also learn to sort objects using the words *same* and *different,* and to group objects according to different attributes. He or she will also decide which objects belong to a group based on characteristics such as color, shape, size, and kind.

You can encourage your child to learn these concepts by doing the following activities together.

_____

Matched and Mismatched

Materials socks, shoes, hats, other clothing items; two boxes or laundry baskets

Step 1 Select five or six different articles of clothing and lay them out on a table.

Step 2 Invite your child to pick out two similar items and explain how they are different and how they are the same. Encourage him or her to talk about the sizes, shapes, and colors of the items. Repeat the activity several times.

Step 3 Have the child put the items on using various rules for *same* and *different.* For example, you might ask your child to put on two socks of the same color and two shoes of different colors.

Find the Odd Item

Materials a collection of toys or other household objects

While the child is out of the room, place four or five similar objects on the table. Add an object that clearly does not belong. For example, you might add a baseball to a group of toy cars and trucks. Then ask your child to pick out the object that doesn't belong and describe why. Talk with your child about the objects in the group. What makes them the same? What makes the object that doesn't belong different?

Posición y clasificación

Estimada familia:

En este capítulo, su hijo/a aprenderá a describir la posición de objetos usando palabras y frases como *encima, debajo, sobre, adentro, afuera, a la izquierda, a la derecha, arriba, en el medio* y *abajo.* Su hijo/a también aprenderá a clasificar objetos usando las palabras *igual/mismo* y *diferente,* y a agrupar objetos de acuerdo con diferentes atributos. También deberá decidir qué objetos pertenecen a un grupo basándose en características como color, forma, tamaño y clase.

Usted puede ayudar a su hijo/a a aprender estos conceptos haciendo juntos las actividades que se describen a continuación.

Parejo y desparejo

Materiales medias, zapatos, sombreros, otras prendas de vestir; dos cajas o canastos para la ropa

Primer paso Seleccione cinco o seis prendas de vestir diferentes y colóquelas sobre una mesa.

Segundo paso Pídale a su hijo/a que elija dos objetos similares y que explique en qué se diferencian y en qué se parecen. Pídale que hable sobre los tamaños, las formas y los colores de los objetos. Repita la actividad varias veces.

Tercer paso Pídale que se ponga las distintas prendas usando distintas reglas de *igual/mismo* y *diferente.* Por ejemplo, le puede pedir que se ponga dos medias del mismo color o dos zapatos de colores diferentes.

Busca el objeto que no pertenece al grupo

Materiales un conjunto de juguetes u otros objetos de la casa

Sin que su hijo/a vea lo que usted está haciendo, coloque cuatro o cinco objetos similares sobre la mesa. Añada un objeto que claramente no pertenezca al grupo. Por ejemplo, puede colocar una pelota de béisbol en un grupo de coches y camiones de juguete. Luego pídale a su hijo/a que seleccione el objeto que no pertenece al grupo y que describa por qué. Hable con su hijo/a acerca de los objetos del grupo. ¿En qué se parecen? ¿Por qué es diferente el objeto que no pertenece al grupo?

Name_____

Inside and Outside

Name_____

STUDY BUDDIES 1 COACH'S NOTES

Inside and Outside

Your goal: To help your buddy understand the positions of objects using the words *inside* and *outside.*

I. Tell your buddy that you are going to practice finding things that are inside and outside the box.

2. Ask your buddy, "What is this?" Point to each of the objects shown outside the box. Make sure your buddy identifies the bowl, plate, cup, and fork.

3. Ask your buddy to circle the cup that is inside the box. Watch to see if your buddy understands the word inside.

4. Ask your buddy to circle the plate that is outside the box. Watch to see if your buddy understands the word outside.

5. Continue asking your buddy to circle different objects either inside or outside the box. You might also point to an object and ask if the object is inside or outside the box.

Try this: Throughout your daily activities, reinforce these words and concepts frequently. When you mail something, for example, say, "The letter is outside the mailbox." Then put the letter in the mailbox and say, "Now the letter is inside the mailbox."

STUDY BUDDIES 2 STUDENT PAGE

Sorting the Same Set in Different Ways

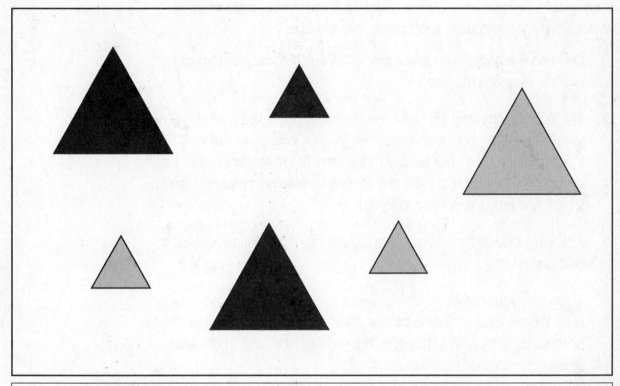

STUDY BUDDIES 2 COACH'S NOTES

Sorting the Same Set in Different Ways

Your goal: To help your buddy practice sorting the same objects using different attributes, such as shape and size.

I. Discuss the shapes on the page with your buddy. Tell him or her each shape is a triangle.

2. Tell your buddy that some of the triangles are large and some are small. Ask your buddy to circle the large triangles in the first box. Watch to see that your buddy circles the 3 large triangles of both colors. Ask which triangles are circled (the large triangles) and which are not (the small triangles).

3. Ask your buddy to tell you what colors the triangles are. (black and gray)

4. Then ask your buddy to circle all the gray triangles in the second box. Watch to see that he or she finds all the gray triangles of both sizes. Ask which triangles are circled (the gray triangles) and which are not (the black triangles).

Try this: Gather small objects with multiple characteristics, such as beans, buttons, or coins. Have your buddy practice sorting the objects. When he or she has sorted them once, ask, if there is another way to sort them.

© Pearson Education, Inc. **K**

Name_____

Graphing and Patterns

Dear Family,

In this chapter, your child will learn about graphing and patterns. He or she will compare groups using a one-to-one correspondence to find which has *as many as, more,* or *fewer* items. Your child will learn to make and read real graphs, picture graphs, and bar graphs. In the pattern section of the chapter, your child will identify and extend sound, color, and shape patterns. He or she will also compare patterns, show a pattern in more than one way, and create patterns.

You can help improve your child's understanding of these concepts by doing the following activities together.

_____

Name That Pattern

Step 1 Make a repeated pattern of sounds and hand motions by clapping your hands, slapping them on your knees, or touching your elbows. For example, you might repeat the sequence clap-clap-slap several times.

Step 2 Ask your child to try and imitate the sequence and also to describe it in words.

Step 3 Give your child a turn at making up a pattern for you to describe and perform.

Patterns, Numbers, Graphs

Materials a collection of patterned natural objects, like leaves, flowers, seeds or nuts, snail shells

Step 1 Have your child describe the various patterns on the objects.

Step 2 Have your child draw one or two of the patterns, like the veins on a leaf or the swirls on a shell.

Step 3 Invite your child to pick two object and guess which one is more common in nature. Then have him or her make a drawing that shows this. For example, a child who guesses that leaves are more common than seeds might draw five leaves and two seeds.

CARTA A LA FAMILIA

Gráficas y patrones

Estimada familia:

En este capítulo, su hijo/a aprenderá acerca de gráficas y patrones. Comparará grupos usando una correspondencia de uno a uno para averiguar cuál tiene *la misma cantidad de* objetos, *más* objetos o *menos* objetos. Su hijo aprenderá a hacer y a interpretar gráficas reales, gráficas con dibujos y gráficas de barras. En la sección de este capítulo dedicada a los patrones, su hijo/a identificará y extenderá patrones de sonidos, colores y formas. También comparará patrones, mostrará un patrón de más de una manera y creará patrones.

Usted puede ayudar a su hijo/a a comprender mejor estos conceptos haciendo juntos las actividades que se describen a continuación.

Nombra ese patrón

Primer paso Haga un patrón repetido de sonidos y movimientos de las manos aplaudiendo, golpeando las manos contra las rodillas o tocándose los codos. Por ejemplo, puede repetir varias veces la secuencia aplauso-aplauso-aplauso.

Segundo paso Pídale a su hijo/a que trate de imitar la secuencia y que también la describa con palabras.

Tercer paso Pídale a su hijo/a que invente un patrón para que usted lo describa y repita.

Patrones, números y gráficas

Materiales un conjunto de objetos naturales con patrones, como hojas de plantas, flores, semillas o nueces, y caracoles

Primer paso Pídale a su hijo/a que describa los distintos patrones que vea en los objetos.

Segundo paso Pídale a su hijo/a que dibuje uno o dos de los patrones, como las nervaduras de una hoja o los espirales de un caracol.

Tercer paso Pídale a su hijo/a que elija dos objetos y adivine cuál es más común en la naturaleza. Luego pídale que haga un dibujo que muestre eso. Por ejemplo, un niño que cree que las hojas son más comunes que las semillas podría dibujar cinco hojas y dos semillas.

STUDY BUDDIES 3 STUDENT PAGE

Bar Graphs

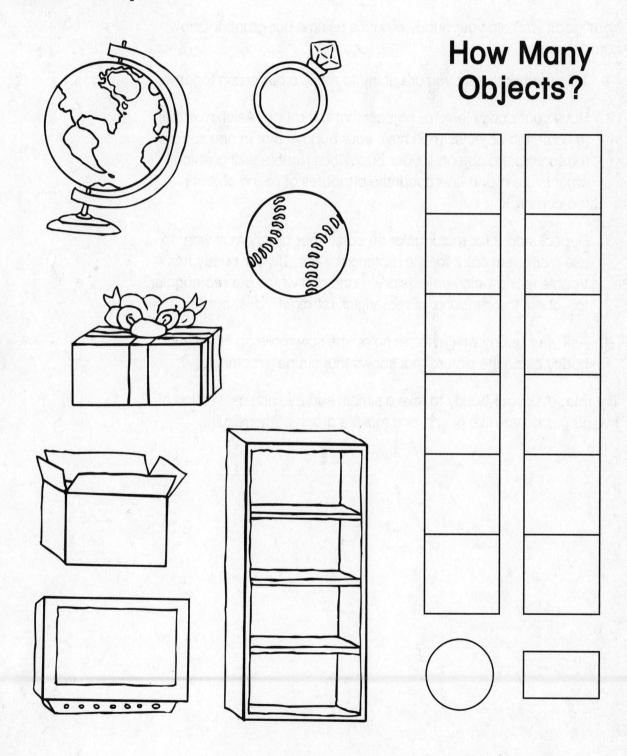

How Many Objects?

Name_____

STUDY BUDDIES 3 COACH'S NOTES

Bar Graphs

Your goal: To help your buddy practice using a bar graph to show comparisons.

1. Tell your buddy that you are going to make a bar graph together.

2. Have your buddy look for objects that are round. Ask him or her to name the objects. Then have your buddy color in one square for each round object. If your buddy has trouble telling which objects are round, talk about the attributes of round objects (no corners).

3. Repeat step 2 for rectangular objects. Your buddy may want to use a different color for the rectangular bar. If your buddy has trouble telling which objects are round and which are rectangular, talk about the attributes of rectangles (straight sides, corners).

4. Ask your buddy which shape he or she saw more of. Have your buddy circle the picture that shows that shape. (rectangle)

Try this: Ask your buddy to take a simple survey such as, "Which of two games do you like best?" and make a graph of the results.

Name_____

STUDY BUDDIES 4 STUDENT PAGE

Shape Patterns

❶

❷

❸

Name_____

Shape Patterns

Your goal: To help your buddy practice identifying the pattern and choosing the next shape.

1. Tell your buddy that you are going to look at some patterns and decide what comes next.

2. Have your buddy put his or her finger on each shape in pattern 1 as you say the shape's name. (flower, star, flower, star, etc.)

3. Ask your buddy which shape comes next. Have your buddy circle the correct shape. The next shape is a flower.

4. Repeat with pattern 2. Pay attention to how your buddy approaches the pattern. Help him or her to identify the sequence of the shapes that repeat. The next shape is a square.

5. Repeat with pattern 3. The third pattern has a recurring shape. If he or she needs help identifying the pattern, have your buddy point to each shape and say its name. Then help your buddy see that two stars always follow the circle. The next shape is a star.

Try this: Look for shape patterns in your daily activities. Show the pattern to your buddy and ask which shape would come next.

Name _____

FAMILY LETTER

CHAPTER 3

Numbers Through 5

Dear Family,

Your child is learning numbers through 5 in this chapter. He or she will count objects, write the numerals, and read number words. The quantity 0 will also be introduced. He or she will order the numbers 0 to 5 and use the words *first* through *fifth* to describe ordinal positions.

You can help develop your child's understanding of the numbers 0 through 5 by doing the following activities together.

More or Fewer?

Materials marbles, hairpins, pennies, or other small, identical objects; two plates

Step 1 Put 2 objects on one plate and 3 on the other. Ask your child to tell you which plate has more objects on it, and which has fewer.

Step 2 Lay out different combinations of up to 5 objects on each of the two plates. Again, ask your child which plate has more, and which has fewer.

Step 3 Try the following variation. Put 3 items on one plate, then tell the child to put more (or fewer) items on the other plate.

Name that Number

Materials two number cubes (from a board game)

Step 1 Have your child roll both cubes and then pick the cube that has more (or fewer) dots showing. Do this several times.

Step 2 Name a number and ask your child to point to a number cube face that has the named number of dots. Again, do this several times.

Step 3 Ask your child to explain what a cube would look like that had the number 0 shown on one face.

CARTA A LA FAMILIA

Los números hasta el 5

Estimada familia:

En este capítulo, su hijo/a aprenderá los números hasta el 5. Contará objetos, escribirá los números y leerá los nombres de los números. También se presentará la cantidad 0. Su hijo/a ordenará los números del 0 al 5 y usará las palabras *primero* a *quinto* para describir las posiciones ordinales.

Usted puede ayudar a su hijo/a a desarrollar la comprensión de los números del 0 al 5 haciendo juntos las actividades que se describen a continuación.

¿Más o menos?

Materiales canicas, horquillas para el cabello, monedas u otros objetos pequeños que sean idénticos; dos platos

Primer paso Coloque 2 objetos en un plato y 3 en el otro. Pregúntele a su hijo/a cuál de los dos platos tiene más objetos y cuál tiene menos.

Segundo paso Coloque distintas combinaciones de hasta 5 objetos en cada uno de los platos. Nuevamente, pídale a su hijo/a que le diga qué plato tiene más y qué plato tiene menos.

Tercer paso Pruebe a hacer la siguiente variación. Coloque 3 objetos en un plato y luego pídale a su hijo/a que coloque más (o menos) objetos en el otro plato.

Nombra ese número

Materiales dos dados (de un juego de mesa)

Primer paso Pídale a su hijo/a que arroje los dos dados y que elija el que muestra más (o menos) puntos. Hágalo varias veces.

Segundo paso Diga un número y pídale a su hijo/a que le muestre la cara del dado que tiene ese número de puntos. Repítalo varias veces.

Tercer paso Pídale a su hijo/a que le diga cómo se vería un dado que muestra el número 0 en una cara.

Name_____

STUDY BUDDIES 5 STUDENT PAGE

Counting 1, 2, and 3

 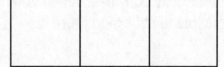

 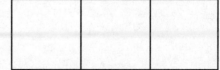

Name_____

STUDY BUDDIES 5 COACH'S NOTES

Counting 1, 2, and 3

Your goal: To help your buddy practice counting the quantities 1, 2, and 3.

1. Tell your buddy that you are going to practice counting together.

2. Ask your buddy to point to a rabbit. Ask how many rabbits he or she can find. (2) Have your buddy color in one square for each rabbit in the picture.

3. Repeat with the bird. Ask your buddy how many birds he or she can find. (1) Have your buddy color in a square for the bird.

4. Repeat with the three deer and two turtles. Tell your buddy that each animal should be counted only once. Ask your buddy how he or she can be sure no animal gets counted more than once. Your buddy could put an "x" on each animal as it is counted.

5. Ask your buddy to count the colored squares for each animal and tell you how many there are for each. Suggest that your study buddy start at the bottom and count up.

Try this: Give your buddy lots of opportunities to practice counting small numbers during your daily activities. When you make a sandwich, ask how many pieces of bread there are.

STUDY BUDDIES 6 STUDENT PAGE

Comparing Numbers Through 5

⭐ **1**

2

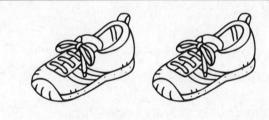

3

Name_____

STUDY BUDDIES 6 COACH'S NOTES

Comparing Numbers Through 5

Your goal: To help your buddy practice comparing groups and determine which has more and which has fewer.

I. Tell your buddy that you are going to compare groups and decide which group has more objects in it.

2. Look at problem I together. Ask your buddy to count the apples and write the number on the line. (4)

3. Then have your buddy count the bananas and write that number. (3)

4. Ask your buddy which group has more. Have your buddy draw a line between one apple and one banana until there aren't any more that match. Then have your buddy circle the group that has more. (apples)

5. Repeat with problem 2. Make sure your buddy recognizes that the first group is not always the largest. (Socks are more.)

6. Repeat with problem 3. Point out to your buddy that sometimes the larger group has more than one object left over. (Bees are 2 more.)

Try this: Use spoons and forks to give your buddy practice with comparing numbers. Say, "There are 3 spoons and 5 forks. Are there more spoons or more forks?" Let your buddy use the objects to find the answer by counting.

FAMILY LETTER

CHAPTER 4

Numbers Through 10

Dear Family,

Your child is learning the numbers 6 through 10 in this chapter. He or she will count objects, write the numerals, and read number words. Your child will also order numbers from 0 to 10 and use the words *sixth* through *tenth* to describe ordinal positions. She or he will also compare numbers, determining which is greater, which is less, which is more or less than 5, and which is more or less than 10.

You can help spark your child's interest in numbers by talking about numbers and counting together. Here are some activities you can do together to reinforce his or her understanding.

Neighborhood Numbers

When you are out in your neighborhood, invite your child to look for the numbers 6, 7, 8, 9, and 10 in your surroundings. You might find the numbers on house addresses, license plates, street signs, and so on.

Button Count

Materials 10 buttons

Step 1 Count out 10 buttons onto a table, and ask your child to make two piles with the 10 buttons. Count aloud the buttons in each pile to find the total in the whole group with your child.

Step 2 Ask which pile has fewer buttons.

Step 3 Repeat Steps 1 and 2 with a different number of buttons in each pile.

Step 4 When your child seems confident, try playing this variation. Put a certain number of buttons in one pile, then tell the child to put more (or fewer) buttons in another pile.

CARTA A LA FAMILIA

Los números hasta el 10

Estimada familia:,

En este capítulo, su hijo/a aprenderá los números del 6 al 10. Contará objetos, escribirá los números y leerá los nombres de los números. Su hijo también ordenará los números del 0 al 10 y usará las palabras *sexto* a *décimo* para describir las posiciones ordinales. También comparará números y deberá determinar cuál es mayor, cuál es menor, cuál es mayor o menor que 5 y cuál es mayor o menor que 10.

Usted puede ayudar a que su hijo/a se interese en los números hablando sobre números y contando juntos. A continuación encontrará algunas actividades que pueden hacer juntos para reforzar la comprensión numérica de su hijo/a.

Números en el barrio

Cuando paseen por su barrio, pídale a su hijo/a que busque los números 6, 7, 8, 9 y 10 en los alrededores. Quizá los encuentre en los números de las casas, en las matrículas de automóviles, en los carteles con los nombres de las calles, etc.

Contar botones

Materiales 10 botones

Primer paso Cuente 10 botones sobre la mesa y pídale a su hijo/a que haga dos pilas con los 10 botones. Cuente los botones de cada pila en voz alta con su hijo para hallar el número total de todo el grupo.

Segundo paso Pregúntele a su hijo/a cuál de los dos grupos tiene menos botones.

Tercer paso Repita el primer paso y el segundo paso con un número diferente de botones en cada pila.

Cuarto paso Cuando parezca que su hijo/a ya domina la actividad, intente esta variación. Ponga un cierto número de botones en una pila, y pídale a su hijo que ponga más (o menos) botones en otra pila.

Name_____

STUDY BUDDIES 7 STUDENT PAGE

Reading and Writing 6, 7, and 8

⭐1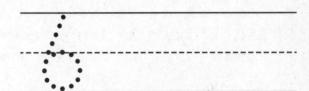

🍎2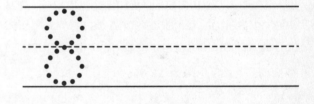

❸3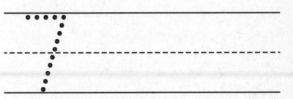

STUDY BUDDIES 7 COACH'S NOTES

Reading and Writing 6, 7, and 8

Your goal: To help your buddy practice identifying, counting, and writing the numbers 6, 7, and 8.

1. Tell your buddy that you are going to practice counting together.

2. Ask your buddy to look at the pieces of pizza. Count them aloud together. Suggest that your buddy point to each piece as you count.

3. Then watch as your buddy traces the 6. Tell your buddy to practice writing the 6 two more times.

4. Repeat with problem 2. Remind your buddy to start the 8 in the upper right, then move left to start writing the numeral.

5. For problem 3, encourage your buddy to count the flowers independently and then practice writing the numeral.

Try this: Counting and writing numbers are important basic skills. Use household objects such as socks, buttons, and books to give your buddy practice counting and writing numbers through 8.

Name_____

STUDY BUDDIES 8 STUDENT PAGE

Comparing Numbers Through 10

⭐ 1

_____
- - - - - - - - -
_____
- - - - - - - - -
_____

② 2

_____
- - - - - - - - -
_____
- - - - - - - - -
_____

③ 3

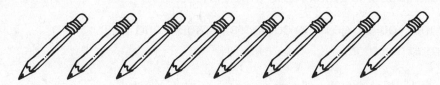

_____
- - - - - - - - -
_____
_____
- - - - - - - - -
_____

STUDY BUDDIES 8 COACH'S NOTES

Comparing Numbers Through 10

Your goal: To help your buddy practice comparing numbers through 10, determining which number is greater and which is less.

1. Tell your buddy that you are going to compare numbers and decide which group has more.

2. Ask your buddy to look at the pencils and crayons. Have your buddy draw a line between one pencil and one crayon until there are not enough left in one group to match. Ask which group has more. Have your buddy circle the group with more. (pencils)

3. Then have your buddy count the items in each group (8 pencils and 6 crayons) and write the number on the line. Ask which group has more. Then have your buddy circle the greater number. (8)

4. Repeat the steps with problem 2. Count the items in each group together, pointing to each object as you go to help your buddy keep track of which objects have been counted. (7 dogs and 10 collars.)

5. Repeat the steps with problem 3. (9 shirts and 8 caps.) Explain to your buddy that when you draw lines to match items between groups, sometimes there will be more than one left over in the larger group, and sometimes there will be just one left over in the larger group.

Try this: When you grocery shop, use the items you buy to give your buddy practice counting and comparing numbers. Ask your buddy questions such as which is more, 8 apples or 6 oranges.

© Pearson Education, Inc. K

FAMILY LETTER   **CHAPTER 5**

Numbers Through 31

Dear Family,

Your child is learning about numbers up to 31, including how to recognize, write, read the number word, order, and compare them in terms of *more* and *fewer*. He or she is also learning to skip count by 2s and by 5s, and estimate the quantities of groups based on visual comparisons.

You can help develop your child's skill with larger numbers by talking about them and doing the following activities together.

Guess the Number

Play the following game with your child. One person announces that he or she is thinking of a number in a certain range, and the other person has to guess the number. For example, one player could start by saying, "I'm thinking of a number between 15 and 22." Don't worry too much about the size of the intervals, so long as they are not unreasonably large or small. Clues can be given if the number is lower or higher than the guess. Play until the correct number is found, and then reverse roles.

Skip Counting

Materials 30 beans or other set of identical objects

Step 1 Place the beans on a table and count them aloud with your child, one at a time.

Step 2 Now start over with all beans together. Have the child slide 2 beans to the side, while you say "two." Have the child slide over 2 more, while you say "four," and continue in this fashion until you have counted all 30 by 2s. Then repeat this step with the roles reversed.

Step 3 Go through Step 2 again, but this time count by 5s. Again, first count while your child moves beans, then move beans while your child counts.

123 CARTA A LA FAMILIA   **Capítulo 5**

Los números hasta el 31

Estimada familia:

En este capítulo, su hijo/a aprenderá los números hasta el 31, incluyendo cómo reconocer, escribir y leer el nombre de cada número, cómo ordenarlos y cómo compararlos en términos de *más* y *menos*. También aprenderá a contar de 2 en 2 y de 5 en 5, y a estimar las cantidades de grupos basándose en comparaciones visuales.

Usted puede ayudar a su hijo/a a desarrollar las habilidades con números grandes hablando sobre los números y haciendo juntos las actividades que se describen a continuación.

Adivina el número

Juegue el siguiente juego con su hijo/a. Una persona anuncia que está pensando en un número en cierto rango y la otra persona tiene que adivinar el número. Por ejemplo, un jugador puede comenzar diciendo: "Estoy pensando en un número entre 15 y 22". No se preocupe demasiado por el tamaño de los intervalos de números, siempre que no sean demasiado grandes o demasiado pequeños. Se pueden dar pistas si el número es mayor o menor que el número que sugiere el jugador que adivina. Juegue hasta hallar el número correcto, y luego juegue otra vez invirtiendo los roles.

Contar salteado

Materiales 30 frijoles u otro juego de objetos idénticos

Primer paso Coloque los frijoles sobre una mesa y cuéntelos en voz alta con su hijo/a, uno por uno.

Segundo paso Ahora comience nuevamente con todos los frijoles juntos. Pídale a su hijo/a que deslice 2 frijoles hacia el costado mientras usted dice "dos". Pídale a su hijo que deslice 2 más mientras usted dice "cuatro" y continúe de esta manera hasta haber contado los 30 frijoles de 2 en 2. Luego repita este paso con los roles invertidos.

Tercer paso Vuelva a repetir el paso 2, pero hágalo contando de 5 en 5. Nuevamente, cuente usted primero mientras su hijo/a desliza los frijoles, y luego deslice los frijoles usted mientras su hijo/a cuenta.

STUDY BUDDIES 9 STUDENT PAGE

Counting 11 to 20

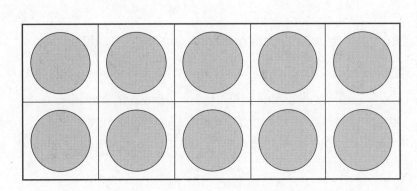

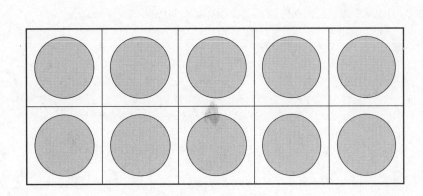

Name_____

STUDY BUDDIES 9 COACH'S NOTES

Counting 11 to 20

Your goal: To help your buddy practice counting numbers from 11 through 20.

1. Have 20 counters or small objects available for your buddy to use for counting.

2. Have your buddy use counters or objects to count and model the numbers 11 through 15 on the top diagram. Count each number out loud with your buddy. Make sure your buddy uses the spaces inside the ten frame first.

3. Then have your buddy choose one number from 11 through 15 to show. Have him or her count and model the number. Make sure your buddy draws and colors enough extra counters on the top diagram to show the number.

4. Use the second diagram to repeat steps 2 and 3 with any number from 16 through 20.

Try this: Find as many chances as possible in your daily activities for your buddy to practice counting. Count cars passing your house, people in a store, books on a shelf, and so on, together.

Name_____

STUDY BUDDIES 10 STUDENT PAGE

Comparing Numbers Through 31

1

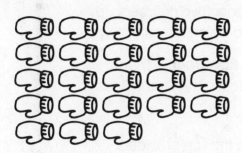

_____   _____

- - - - - - - - - -   - - - - - - - - - -

2

_____   _____

- - - - - - - - - -   - - - - - - - - - -

3

_____   _____

- - - - - - - - - -   - - - - - - - - - -

Name_____

STUDY BUDDIES 10 COACH'S NOTES

Comparing Numbers Through 31

Your goal: To help your buddy practice comparing two numbers up through 31, finding which number is greater and which is less.

1. Ask your buddy to count the mittens in the first group. (There are 23.) Encourage your buddy to count aloud if he or she finds it helpful.

2. Then have your buddy write the number on the line provided. Watch to see that he or she writes the digits correctly and in the correct order.

3. Repeat steps one and two with the second group. Again, encourage your buddy to count aloud. (There are 19 mittens.)

4. Ask your buddy which number is less. Have your buddy circle the lesser number. (19) If your buddy is unsure, ask your buddy which number comes first when you count up from 1.

5. Use the other two problems for additional practice. You can vary the exercise by asking your buddy to circle the greater number instead of the lesser number. (There are 18 apples and 15 strawberries in problem 2, and 27 stars and 26 rockets in problem 3.)

Try this: On a visit to a park or beach, collect a number of rocks, leaves, or other small objects. Make groups of the objects and ask your buddy to count them and tell you which is the greater or lesser number.

© Pearson Education, Inc. **K**

FAMILY LETTER

CHAPTER 6

Measurement

Dear Family,

Your child is studying measurement in this chapter. He or she will compare objects by their size and length, and order containers based on their volume. Using nonstandard units, your child will also measure length, capacity and weight of objects. He or she will also explore temperatures (hot or cold) on a thermometer.

You can foster your child's grasp of measurement concepts by comparing things throughout the day, using words like *bigger* and *smaller, shorter* and *longer, more* and *less,* and *hotter* and *colder.* Here are some activities that will give you a chance to do this.

Measuring by Stacking

Materials various measurable objects, such as a crayon, a CD case, a drinking cup, a spoon, a stack of identical wooden blocks, or books of similar thickness

Step 1 Have your child measure a couple of objects against the stack of blocks or books, rounding to the nearest unit. A crayon, for instance, might be 2 blocks long. Record the measurements.

Step 2 Ask your child to estimate the size of the other objects, then check by measuring.

Kitchen Math

Materials 3 or 4 small cooking and baking containers (preferably metal or plastic) of different sizes and shapes

Step 1 Ask your child to think of a way to tell which container holds more water. Guide your child toward the idea of filling one container, then pouring the contents into another to see whether the second container has space left, overflows, or is exactly filled.

Step 2 Have your child use that technique to order the containers from the smallest capacity to the largest capacity. Talk about whether the largest-capacity container always has to be the tallest one. (It doesn't.)

Medición

Estimada familia:

En este capítulo, su hijo/a estudiará la medición. Comparará objetos según el tamaño y la longitud, y ordenará recipientes según el volumen. Usando medidas no estándar, su hijo/a también medirá la longitud, la capacidad y el peso de objetos. También explorará las temperaturas del termómetro (caliente o frío).

Usted puede ayudar a su hijo/a a comprender los conceptos de medición comparando objetos en forma cotidiana, usando palabras y frases como *más grande* y *más pequeño, más corto* y *más largo, más* y *menos,* y *más caliente* y *más frío.* A continuación se describen algunas actividades para practicar estos conceptos.

Medir armando pilas

Materiales distintos objetos medibles, como un crayón, una caja de CD, una taza, un vaso; una pila de bloques de madera idénticos, o libros de grosores similares.

Primer paso Pídale a su hijo/a que mida un par de objetos contra la pila de bloques o libros, redondeando hasta la unidad más cercana. Por ejemplo, un crayón puede medir 2 bloques de largo.

Segundo paso Pídale a sus hijos que estimen el tamaño de otros objetos, y luego verifiquen las estimaciones haciendo la medición.

Matemáticas en la cocina

Materiales 3 ó 4 recipientes de cocina (preferentemente de metal o de plástico) de diferentes formas y tamaños.

Primer paso Pídale a su hijo/a que piense en una manera de comprobar en cuál de los recipientes cabe más agua. Guíe a su hijo/a hacia la idea de llenar un recipiente, luego verter el contenido en otro para ver si queda espacio en el segundo recipiente, si rebalsa o si se llena hasta el borde.

Segundo paso Pídale a su hijo/a que use esa técnica para ordenar los recipientes desde el que tiene menor capacidad hasta el que tiene mayor capacidad. Hable acerca de si el recipiente de mayor capacidad siempre tiene que ser el más alto. (No tiene por qué serlo.)

STUDY BUDDIES 11 STUDENT PAGE

Ordering by Length

STUDY BUDDIES 11 COACH'S NOTES

Ordering by Length

Your goal: To help your buddy practice ordering objects by length from shortest to longest.

I. Tell your buddy that you will be practicing putting the flowers in order by their length. Let your buddy pick two colors of crayons. (Your buddy may use any colors he or she likes, but for clarity, these directions will use red and blue.)

2. Ask your buddy which flower is the tallest flower. Watch to see that he or she points to the flower on the left. Have your buddy color that flower blue.

3. Then ask which flower is the shortest. Watch to see that he or she indicates the middle flower. Have your buddy color that flower red.

4. Ask your buddy to name the three flowers in order from shortest to tallest (red, white, blue).

Try this: Find three pencils or pens of different lengths, or break a piece of uncooked spaghetti into three unequal pieces. Ask your buddy to show you the objects in order from shortest to longest. Repeat with different objects, also ordering them from longest to shortest.

© Pearson Education, Inc. **K**

Name_____

STUDY BUDDIES 12 STUDENT PAGE

Comparing and Ordering by Weight

1

2

3

Name_____

Comparing and Ordering by Weight

Your goal: To help your buddy practice comparing and ordering objects by their weights.

1. Tell your buddy that you will be practicing finding the heaviest and lightest objects in a group.

2. Direct your buddy's attention to problem 1. Ask, "Which is heaviest?" (the bicycle) Tell your buddy to circle the heaviest object.

3. Then ask, "Which is lightest?" (the piece of paper) Ask your buddy to mark an X on the lightest object.

4. Ask your buddy to point to and name the three objects in order from lightest to heaviest. (paper, kitten, bicycle)

5. Repeat the steps to help your buddy name the objects in problems 2 and 3 in lightest to heaviest order. (envelope, waste basket, table), (penny, box of cereal, person)

Try this: When you shop, use your purchases to let your buddy practice comparing objects by weight. Groceries and other types of purchases (clothing, office supplies, etc.) provide good practice.

FAMILY LETTER

CHAPTER 7

Time and Money

Dear Family,

In this chapter, your child will learn how to use the words *yesterday, today,* and *tomorrow* to place events in order, how to distinguish morning, afternoon, and evening, and how to tell time to the nearest hour. Your child will also learn the days of the week and the months and seasons of the year. Finally, he or she will learn about the values of pennies, nickels, dimes, quarters, and dollars.

Here are some activities you can do with your child to strengthen his or her grasp of these concepts.

_____

Current Events

Talk about family events that are going on right now, and have your child put together a sequential description using *yesterday, today,* and *tomorrow* as well as *morning, afternoon,* and *evening.* The narrative should start with, "Yesterday morning, I (or we) ..." and finish with, "Tomorrow evening...." If your child enjoys drawing, let him or her draw illustrations for the story.

Mock Market

Materials Pennies, nickels, dimes, quarters, and a dollar bill or two; some items for "purchase" such as pieces of fruit, small toys, costume jewelry, or books.

Step 1 Use masking tape to label each item with a price: 1¢, 5¢, 10¢, 25¢, or $1. You may also want to label a couple of items with other prices, such as 7¢ or 35¢.

Step 2 Play "market" with your child, with you as the seller. Start by having your child buy one of the lower-priced items using a single coin.

Step 3 Buy the item back from the child, using the same coin. Then have the child buy the same item again, using a combination of other coins (2 nickels to buy a 10-cent item).

Step 4 Continue the market game, using different combinations of coins (such as 3 dimes and a nickel to buy a 35-cent item).

CARTA A LA FAMILIA

Tiempo y dinero

Estimada familia:

En este capítulo, su hijo/a aprenderá a usar las palabras *ayer, hoy* y *mañana* para ordenar acontecimientos, aprenderá a distinguir la mañana, la tarde y la noche, y aprenderá a decir la hora redondeando a la hora más cercana. Su hijo/a también aprenderá los días de la semana y los meses y las estaciones del año. Por último, aprenderá acerca de los valores de las monedas de 1 centavo, 5 centavos, 10 centavos, 25 centavos y los dólares.

A continuación encontrará algunas actividades que puede hacer con su hijo/a para ayudarle a comprender estos conceptos.

Acontecimientos actuales

Hable acerca de acontecimientos familiares que estén teniendo lugar actualmente y pídale a su hijo/a que los describa en una secuencia usando las palabras *ayer, hoy* y *mañana* y también *mañana, tarde* y *noche.* La narración debe comenzar con "Ayer a la mañana yo (o nosotros)..." y terminar con "Mañana por la noche..." Si a su hijo/a le gusta dibujar, pídale que ilustre la historia.

Jugar a ir de compras

Materiales Monedas de 1 centavo, 5 centavos, 10 centavos y 25 centavos y uno o dos billetes de un dólar; algunos objetos para "comprar", como frutas, juguetes pequeños, joyas de juguete o libros.

Primer paso Use cinta adhesiva de papel para ponerle un precio a cada artículo: 1¢, 5¢, 10¢, 25¢ o $1. También puede ponerle otros precios a un par de objetos, por ejemplo 7¢ o 35¢.

Segundo paso Juegue a ir de compras con su hijo/a. Haga usted el papel del vendedor. Comience pidiéndole a su hijo/a que compre uno de los objetos más baratos usando una sola moneda.

Tercer paso Cómprele usted el mismo objeto a su hijo/a, usando la misma moneda. Luego pídale que vuelva a comprar el mismo objeto, usando una combinación de otras monedas (por ejemplo, 2 monedas de 5 centavos para comprar un objeto que vale 10 centavos).

Cuarto paso Siga jugando a ir de compras usando diferentes combinaciones de monedas (por ejemplo, 3 monedas de 10 centavos y una moneda de 5 centavos para comprar un objeto de 35 centavos).

STUDY BUDDIES 13 STUDENT PAGE

Ordering Events

_____   _____   _____

- - - - - - - - -   - - - - - - - - -   - - - - - - - - -

_____   _____   _____

_____   _____   _____

- - - - - - - - -   - - - - - - - - -   - - - - - - - - -

_____   _____   _____

- - - - - - - - -   - - - - - - - - -   - - - - - - - - -

Name_____

STUDY BUDDIES 13 COACH'S NOTES

Ordering Events

Your goal: to help your buddy practice ordering events.

I. Ask your buddy to tell you what is happening in the first row. Listen to be sure that your buddy understands that the child in the pictures is raking leaves.

2. Ask your buddy what would happen first. (the second picture) Have your buddy write the number I beneath that picture.

3. Then ask your buddy what would happen next. (the first picture) Have your buddy write the number 2 beneath that picture.

4. Then ask your buddy what would happen last. (the third picture) Have your buddy write the number 3 beneath that picture. Then ask your buddy to point to the pictures in order.

5. Repeat the steps with the next two rows of pictures. Make sure your buddy understands and can explain what happens first, second, and third in each sequence. (In the second row, the pictures are in the order 3, 1, 2. In the third row, the order is 1, 3, 2.)

Try this: When you are about to do something that requires two or three steps, ask your buddy in what order you should do them. Use simple activities your buddy might do everyday.

© Pearson Education, Inc. **K**

STUDY BUDDIES 14 STUDENT PAGE

Nickel

      3¢   6¢   7¢

      4¢   5¢   9¢

   2¢   6¢   7¢

STUDY BUDDIES 14 COACH'S NOTES

Nickel

Your goal: to help your buddy practice finding the value of combinations of coins that include nickels.

1. Ask your buddy to point to the nickel in the first row. Ask how many cents a nickel is worth. (5¢)

2. Next, ask your buddy how many pennies there are. (2)

3. Have your buddy put his or her finger on the nickel and count 5 cents. Then have him or her point to each penny and count 1 more cent each time. Ask how many cents there are in all. (7¢)

4. Ask your buddy to circle the correct amount.

5. Repeat the steps for the middle row. If your buddy counts the number of coins instead of their value, remind him or her that a nickel is worth 5 cents. Remind your buddy to count on from the nickel: 5¢, 6¢, 7¢, 8¢, 9¢.

6. Go through the same steps for the bottom row. To double-check your buddy's thought process, ask how much the nickel and penny are each worth. (5¢, 1¢) Your buddy should circle 6¢.

Try this: When you receive nickels and pennies as change, ask your buddy to count the change for you. For example, if you pay with two $1 bills for something that costs $1.93, ask your buddy to count the 7 cents change.

FAMILY LETTER

CHAPTER 8

Geometry and Fractions

Dear Family,

In this chapter, your child will be studying geometry and fractions. He or she will learn to identify and describe plane shapes: circles, rectangles, squares, and triangles; and solid shapes: spheres, cylinders, cubes, and cones. Your child will combine shapes to make new shapes and determine if a position of a shape has changed because the shape has made a flip, slide, or turn. Your child will also study fractions and learn if shapes are symmetric, have equal parts, or are divided into halves or fourths.

Here are some activities you can do with your child to strengthen his or her grasp of these concepts.

I Spy a Shape

Take a tour of your home. When you spot a shape, announce it with "I spy." For example, you might see a soup can and say, "I spy a cylinder." Then have your child guess what you're looking at. Then it becomes his or her turn to "I spy" a shape and let you guess. Make sure your child is using the correct terms, such as *sphere* instead of "ball."

A Toast to Geometry

Materials Two or more slices of bread, toasted or untoasted; other sandwich fixings

Step 1 Lay two consecutive slices from the same loaf of bread next to each other, and have your child arrange them symmetrically, so that they will align neatly when placed together. Ask your child why this is a good way to make a sandwich. (The ingredients are less likely to fall out.)

Step 2 Have your child make a sandwich and have him or her ask you to cut it into 2 or 3 equal-sized parts. Talk about whether this was easy or hard to do. (It may depend on the shape of the bread slices.)

Step 3 Let your child eat the sandwich!

CARTA A LA FAMILIA　　　　　　　　　　**Capítulo 8**

Geometría y fracciones

Estimada familia:

En este capítulo, su hijo/a aprenderá acerca de geometría y fracciones. Aprenderá a identificar y describir figuras planas: círculos, rectángulos, cuadrados y triángulos; y sólidos geométricos: esferas, cilindros, cubos y conos. Su hijo/a combinará figuras para hacer figuras nuevas y determinará si la posición de una figura ha cambiado porque se ha hecho una reflexión, una traslación o una rotación. Su hijo/a también estudiará fracciones y aprenderá si las figuras son simétricas, tienen partes iguales o están divididas en mitades o cuartos.

A continuación encontrará algunas actividades que puede hacer con su hijo/a para ayudarle a comprender estos conceptos.

_____

Veo, veo una figura

Camine por su casa. Cuando vea una figura, anúnciela diciendo "Veo, veo". Por ejemplo, si ve una lata de refresco puede decir "Veo, veo un cilindro". Luego pídale a su hijo/a que adivine cuál es el objeto que usted está mirando. Después será el turno de que su hijo/a diga "veo, veo" una figura y usted adivine. Asegúrese de que su hijo/a use los términos correctos, como *esfera* en lugar de "bola" o "pelota".

Un sándwich geométrico

Materiales Dos o más rebanadas de pan, tostado o sin tostar; ingredientes para sándwiches

Primer paso Ponga dos rebanadas del mismo pan una junto a la otra, y pídale a su hijo/a que las acomode en forma simétrica para que queden bien alineadas al juntarlas. Pregúntele a su hijo/a por qué ésta es una buena manera de hacer un sándwich. (Es menos probable que los ingredientes se salgan.)

Segundo paso Pídale a su hijo/a que arme un sándwich y dígale que le pida a usted que lo corte en 2 ó 3 partes iguales. Hable acerca de si esto fue fácil o difícil de hacer. (Puede depender de la forma de las rebanadas de pan.)

Tercer paso ¡Deje que su hijo/a se coma el sándwich!

Name_____

STUDY BUDDIES 15 STUDENT PAGE

Squares and Other Rectangles

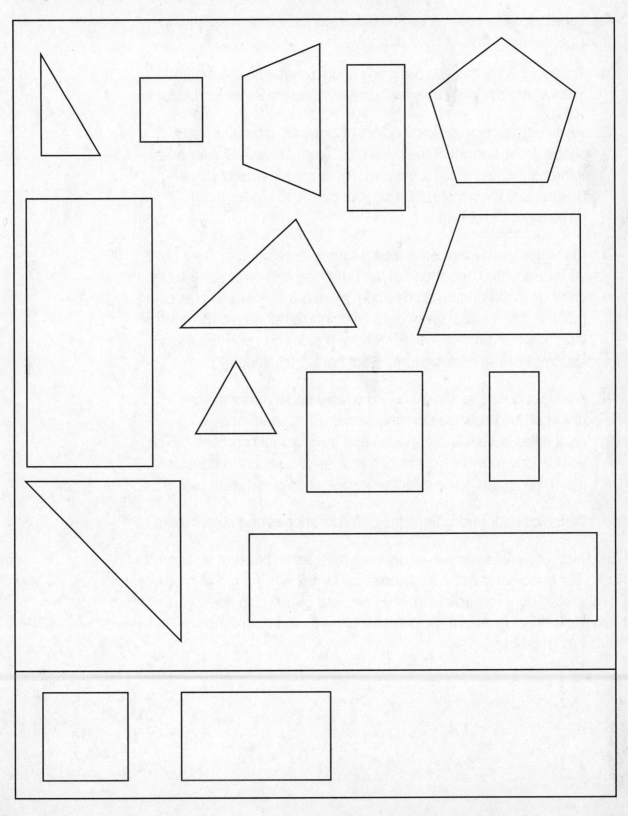

Name_____

STUDY BUDDIES 15 COACH'S NOTES

Squares and Other Rectangles

Your goal: to help your buddy identify squares and rectangles and describe them in terms of their attributes.

1. Tell your buddy that you are going to do a shape puzzle together. You will say a riddle, and your buddy will find the shape and color it.

2. Invite your buddy to pick 2 colors of crayons and color each shape at the bottom of the page a different color. Ask your buddy to name the two shapes. (square, rectangle) If your buddy is unsure, say the names and ask your buddy to repeat them throughout the activity.

3. Make up a riddle that describes a square or rectangle. Then have your buddy find one shape of the right kind and color it the same color as at the bottom of the page. Here are some examples of riddles: "My 4 sides are straight lines, and all sides are the same length. What am I?" (square) "I have 4 sides and corners like a square, but I'm not a square. What am I?" (rectangle)

4. Ask your buddy to explain how a square and a rectangle are different, and how they are the same. (Both squares and rectangles have 4 straight sides and 4 right-angle corners, which your buddy may call square corners. All of a square's sides are the same length, while a rectangle has sides of different lengths.)

5. Watch as your buddy finds the different shapes and colors them.

Try this: Look for examples of squares and rectangles that you can ask your buddy to identify. You can show him or her the top of a box, a cupboard door, or drawer front. Have your buddy also show you examples of squares and rectangles that he or she has found throughout the day.

Equal Parts

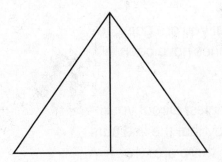 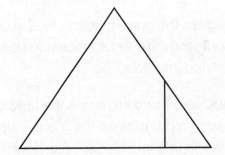

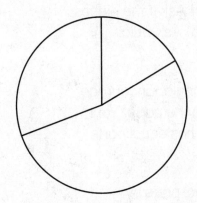 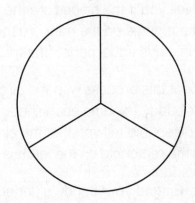

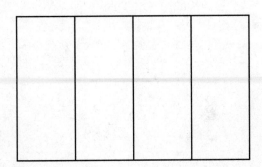 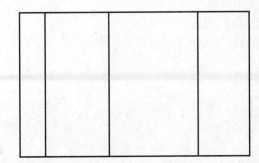

STUDY BUDDIES 16 COACH'S NOTES

Equal Parts

Your goal: to help your buddy recognize shapes that have been divided into two, three, or four equal parts.

I. Look at the page together. Tell your buddy that you are going to compare different shapes and decide which ones have been divided into equal parts.

2. Ask your buddy to name the top figures. (triangles) Direct your buddy's attention to the triangle on the left. Say that the line cuts the triangle into pieces. Ask how many pieces there are. (two) Then ask if the triangle on the right is cut into the same number of pieces. (yes)

3. Ask your buddy to compare the pieces of the triangle on the left and tell you if the pieces are the same size. (yes) Ask if the pieces of the triangle on the right are the same size. (no) Ask which triangle has equal parts. (the triangle on the left)

4. Repeat this process with the circle and the rectangle. Encourage your buddy to name each shape and to describe the parts. Your buddy should tell you that the circle on the right has equal parts and the rectangle on the left has equal parts.

Try this: Extend your buddy's understanding of equal parts by discussing other ways to divide a figure. For example, draw a rectangle and ask your buddy to two draw lines that divide the rectangle into four equal parts.

FAMILY LETTER

CHAPTER 9

Readiness for Addition and Subtraction

Dear Family,

Your child is getting ready to learn about addition and subtraction. Part of getting ready is learning how to build numbers out of lesser numbers—for example, joining 2 objects and 3 objects to make 5 objects. Another part of getting ready is using the concepts *more* and *fewer* with definite quantities: one number is 2 more (1 more, 3 more, ...) than another number.

Help your child prepare for learning about addition and subtraction by doing the following activity together.

Get It Together

Materials 10 buttons (or pennies, or hairpins, or other common objects)

Step 1 Make a pile of buttons (for example, 5 buttons). Count the buttons aloud with your child. Then divide the pile into two piles that differ in number by 1 or 2 buttons (for example, 2 buttons and 3 buttons). Now count the buttons in each pile aloud with your child.

Step 2 Talk with your child about how the buttons are in two groups, but the total is still 5 buttons.

Step 3 Ask your child how many more (or fewer) buttons are in one pile than in the other. To make sure of the answer, the child may want to count the buttons again or spread out the piles side-by-side.

Step 4 As a variation, put a certain number of buttons in a pile, then ask your child to make another pile with 2 more buttons (or 1 more, or 2 fewer, or 1 fewer).

Step 5 Repeat Steps 1 through 4 several times using different numbers.

CARTA A LA FAMILIA

Preparación para la suma y la resta

Estimada familia:

Su hijo se está preparando para aprender acerca de la suma y la resta. Parte de la preparación consiste en aprender a armar números a partir de números más pequeños; por ejemplo, si se juntan 2 objetos y 3 objetos habrá 5 objetos. Otra parte de la preparación consiste en usar los conceptos de *más* y *menos* con cantidades definidas: un número es 2 más (1 más, 3 más, ...) que otro número.

Ayude a su hijo/a a aprender acerca de la suma y la resta haciendo juntos la siguiente actividad.

_____

Pilas y pilas

Materiales 10 botones (o monedas de un centavo, u horquillas para el cabello, u otros objetos comunes)

Primer paso Haga una pila de botones (por ejemplo, 5 botones). Cuente los botones en voz alta con su hijo/a. Luego divida la pila en dos pilas que tengan una diferencia de 1 ó 2 botones (por ejemplo, 2 botones y 3 botones). Luego cuente los botones de cada pila en voz alta con su hijo/a.

Segundo paso Explíquele a su hijo/a que aunque los botones estén en dos grupos el total sigue siendo 5 botones.

Tercer paso Pregúntele a su hijo/a cuántos botones más (o menos) hay en una pila en comparación con la otra. Para asegurarse de la respuesta, su hijo/a puede contar los botones nuevamente o extender las pilas una junto a la otra.

Cuarto paso Como variación, coloque un cierto número de botones en una pila, y luego pídale a su hijo/a que arme otra pila con 2 botones más (o 1 más, o 2 menos, o 1 menos).

Quinto paso Repita del primero al cuarto paso varias veces, usando pilas cada vez más grandes.

STUDY BUDDIES 17 STUDENT PAGE

Ways to Make 4 and 5

Make 4

I and 3

2 and ____

____ and ____

Make 5

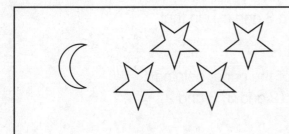

I and 4

2 and ____

____ and 3

____ and ____

Name_____

Ways to Make 4 and 5

Your goal: to help your buddy see the different ways that two numbers or quantities can be combined to make 4 and 5.

1. Tell your buddy that you are going to use colored shapes to build the numbers 4 and 5.

2. Look at top of the page together. Explain that the first box shows one way to build the number 4 by combining two groups of shapes. Have your buddy color the moon one color and the stars another color.

3. Move to the second box. Ask your buddy how many stars are still needed to make a total of 4 shapes in the box. (2) Have your buddy draw those shapes and also fill in the blank with a 2. Then let your buddy color the shapes, using different colors for moons and stars.

4. Move to the third box. Ask your buddy if there is another way to make a total of 4 shapes in the box. (yes) Invite your buddy to describe such a way. (3 moons and 1 star) Have your buddy draw those shapes and also fill in the blanks with a 3 and a 1, in that order. Let your buddy color the shapes.

5. Go through the same steps for the bottom of the page, helping your buddy to find 3 more ways to make 5. (2 and 3, 3 and 2, 4 and 1)

Try this: Ask your buddy whether the order of shapes in the picture has to match the order of shapes in the "and" statement. (no) Can one show 1 and 3 using 1 shape on the right and 3 shapes on the left? (yes) On a separate sheet of paper, encourage your buddy to draw different arrangements to make 4 or 5 shapes in a vertical line.

STUDY BUDDIES 18 STUDENT PAGE

1 Fewer and 2 Fewer

_____

----

1 fewer than 2 is _____.

_____

----

2 fewer than 4 is _____.

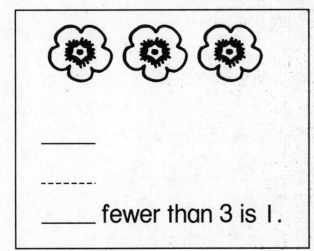

_____

_____ fewer than 3 is 1.

_____   _____

-------   -------

2 fewer than _____ is _____.

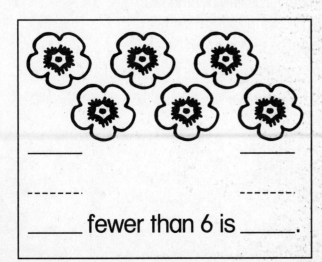

_____   _____

-------   -------

_____ fewer than 6 is _____.

_____   _____

-------   -------

_____ fewer than _____ is _____.

Name_____

 STUDY BUDDIES 18 COACH'S NOTES

I Fewer and 2 Fewer

Your goal: to help your buddy understand the concepts "I fewer" and "2 fewer" as they apply to numbers from 3 to 6.

I. Tell your buddy that you are going to work on understanding "fewer" together by crossing out flowers.

2. Look at the upper left box on the page. Of the 2 flowers, I has been crossed out. Ask your buddy to fill in the blank in the description, so that it describes what is happening to the flowers. (I)

3. Now move to the upper right box. Ask your buddy to finish the box so that the picture and the description match. Suggest looking at the description first and then seeing what needs to be done to the picture. After your buddy crosses out two flowers, he or she should fill in the blank to complete the description. (2)

4. Move to the second row of boxes. Coach your buddy through the description and have him or her count, cross out, and find how many flowers are left.

5. Move to the bottom row of boxes. In the left box, let your buddy choose whether to cross out I or 2 flowers. Make sure the description is filled out to match. Let your buddy fill in the right box with any subtraction problem he or she chooses.

Try this: Talk with your buddy about whether it matters which shapes are crossed out. (no) In the middle right box, does crossing out the first 2 shapes leave the same number of shapes as crossing out the last 2 shapes? (yes) Does the description stay the same either way? (yes)

FAMILY LETTER

CHAPTER 10

Understanding Addition

Dear Family,

Your child is continuing to learn that most numbers can be shown as a combination of two other numbers (part-part-whole). Your child is also learning how to join two groups of different objects to make a larger group. Your child will begin to read symbols, such as plus signs (+), and how to write addition sentences (equations) like $2 + 3 = 5$.

You can help your child understand addition by doing these activities together.

_____

Yours Plus Mine Makes Ours

Materials shoebox; pencil; beans, corn kernels, or other small objects

Step 1 Draw a line down the middle of the shoebox. Say that everything on one side of the line is yours, while everything on the other side is your child's.

Step 2 You and your child take turns dropping up to 10 beans or kernels into the box. Count the things that landed on your side, and say (for instance) "I have 4." Then ask your child to count those that landed on his or her side and name the amount: "I have 6" (for example). Add the two numbers to find the sum. Ask your child to say the result: "We have 10 in all."

A Taste of Arithmetic

Materials two snack foods that come in bite-sized pieces; three pieces of each kind

Step 1 Offer your child two different kinds of snack foods, such as crackers and cheese slices. Tell him or her to take some of each.

Step 2 Tell your child the addition expression for the chosen servings. For example, if the child takes 3 cheese slices and 2 crackers, say, "That's 3 plus 2." Ask your child to tell you the number of pieces in all. When he or she has given the right answer, the snacks may be eaten.

CARTA A LA FAMILIA   **Capítulo 10**

Comprensión de la suma

Estimada familia:

Su hijo/a sigue aprendiendo que casi todos los números pueden mostrarse como una combinación de otros dos números (parte-parte-entero). Su hijo/a también está aprendiendo a unir dos grupos de objetos diferentes para hacer un grupo más grande. Su hijo/a comenzará a leer símbolos, como el signo más (+), y comenzará a escribir oraciones de suma (ecuaciones) como $2 + 3 = 5$.

Usted puede ayudar a su hijo/a a comprender el concepto de suma haciendo juntos las siguientes actividades.

Lo tuyo más lo mío es lo nuestro

Materiales una caja de zapatos; un lápiz; frijoles, semillas de maíz, u otros objetos pequeños

Primer paso Dibuje una línea en el medio de la caja de zapatos. Diga que todo lo que está de un lado es suyo, mientras que todo lo que está del otro lado es de su hijo/a.

Segundo paso Túrnense para dejar caer hasta 10 frijoles o semillas en la caja. Luego cuenten cuántas cosas cayeron del lado de usted y diga (por ejemplo) "Yo tengo 4". Luego pídale a su hijo/a que cuente cuántas cosas cayeron de su lado y diga la cantidad: "Yo tengo 6" (por ejemplo). Sumen los dos números para hallar el total. Pídale a su hijo/a que diga el resultado: "Tenemos 10 en total."

"Snacks" aritméticos

Materiales dos tipos de "snacks" que vengan en pedacitos del tamaño de un bocado; tres de cada uno

Primer paso Ofrézcale a su hijo/a dos tipos diferentes de "snacks", por ejemplo galletitas y rebanadas de queso. Dígale que tome algunos de cada uno.

Segundo paso Dígale a su hijo/a la expresión de suma para los "snacks" que eligió. Por ejemplo, si su hijo/a toma 3 rebanadas de queso y 2 galletitas, diga "Eso es 3 más 2". Pídale a su hijo/a que diga el número total de "snacks". Cuando su hijo/a diga la respuesta correcta, permítale comer los "snacks".

© Pearson Education, Inc. K

STUDY BUDDIES 19 STUDENT PAGE

Joining Groups

_____ and _____ is _____ .

_____ and _____ is _____ .

_____ and _____ is _____ .

Name_____

STUDY BUDDIES 19 COACH'S NOTES

Joining Groups

Your goal: to help your buddy understand the idea of joining two groups of objects together to make a larger group.

I. Tell your buddy that you are going to work on combining groups.

2. Together, look at the top line. Let your buddy count the number of hats on the left and neatly write the number in the first blank. (2)

3. Have your buddy count the number of hats on the right side and write the number in the middle blank. (3)

4. Ask your buddy to draw a loop that includes both groups of hats. Ask your buddy to count the total number of hats and write the number in the last blank. (5) Encourage your buddy to say, "2 and 3 is 5."

5. Do the same steps for the middle row of vehicles. Make sure your buddy draws a loop for the "all together" group, counts and writes the number, and reads the number sentence. (4 and 1 is 5.)

6. Go through the same steps for the bottom row of vegetables. (2 and 5 is 7.)

Try this: Talk about whether it matters which group is on the right and which group is on the left. (no) In the top row, would the total be the same if there were 3 hats on the left and 2 hats on the right? (yes)

STUDY BUDDIES 20 STUDENT PAGE

Using the Plus Sign

_____   _____

----------   ----------

_____   _____

_____   _____

----------   ----------

_____   _____

_____   _____

----------   +   ----------

_____   _____

_____   _____

----------   +   ----------

_____   _____

Name_____

STUDY BUDDIES 20 COACH'S NOTES

Using the Plus Sign

Your goal: to help your buddy use pictures to understand how to use the plus sign.

I. Tell your buddy that you are going to look at pictures together. Explain that he or she will use the plus sign in place of the word *and* to find how many there are in all. You may wish to have your buddy show each number with counters, such as buttons.

2. Look at the top row together. Ask how many elephants there are in the first group. (1) Ask how many elephants there are in the second group. (1) Have your buddy write each number and the plus sign. Ask how many elephants there are in all. (2)

3. Look at the second row. Ask how many crocodiles there are in the first group. (2) Ask how many crocodiles there are in the second group. (2) Have your buddy write each number and the plus sign. Ask how many crocodiles there are in all. (4)

4. Go to the third row. Ask how many pandas there are in the first group. (2) Ask how many pandas there are in the second group. (3) Have your buddy write each number and the plus sign. Ask how many pandas there are in all. (5)

5. Move to the last row. Ask how many gorillas there are in the first group. (4) Ask how many gorillas there are in the second group. (2) Have your buddy write each number and the plus sign. Ask how many gorillas there are in all. (6)

Try this: Ask your buddy what number you get if you combine the number of elephants and the number of crocodiles. (6)

Name_____

FAMILY LETTER

CHAPTER 11

Understanding Subtraction

Dear Family,

Your child is learning to think of subtraction as either a story about separating (for example, "If you start with 5 and take away 2, you have 3 left") or as a story about comparing (for instance, "5 is 2 more than 3"). Your child is learning to use the minus sign ($-$), and to write subtraction sentences (equations), such as $5 - 2 = 3$.

You can help your child understand subtraction by doing these activities together.

_____

It's Out of Sight!

Materials at least 6 socks, cans, wrenches, or other household objects

Step 1 Lay 6 socks on a table. Have your child count and tell how many socks there are.

Step 2 Have your child close his or her eyes while you take away 2 of the socks. Tell your child to look again and say how many socks you took away, and how many socks are left.

Step 3 Repeat Steps 1 and 2 with different numbers, until your child is confident. Then trade roles, so that you count as your child removes socks.

Have It Both Ways

Materials beans, corn kernels, or other small countable objects; paper, pencil

Step 1 On a piece of paper, make blanks for subtraction problems, like this: _____ $-$ _____ $=$ _____

Step 2 Ask your child to place 5 beans on the table, then separate 3 beans from the group. Ask your child to write the subtraction problem, and then say the problem in three different ways: "If you start with 5 and take away 3, you have 2 left"; "5 is 3 more than 2"; and "5 minus 3 equals 2." Repeat using different numbers.

Comprensión de la resta

Estimada familia:

Su hijo/a aprenderá a pensar en la resta como una historia sobre separar (por ejemplo, "Si comienzas con 5 y quitas 2, te quedan 3") o como una historia de comparar (por ejemplo, "5 es 2 más que 3"). Su hijo/a aprenderá a usar el signo menos ($-$), y a escribir oraciones de resta (ecuaciones), como $5 - 2 = 3$.

Usted puede ayudar a su hijo/a a comprender el concepto de resta haciendo juntos las siguientes actividades.

_____

¡No se ven más!

Materiales por lo menos 6 medias, latas, herramientas u otros objetos de la casa

Primer paso Coloque 6 medias sobre una mesa. Pídale a su hijo/a que cuente las medias y le diga cuántas hay.

Segundo paso Pídale a su hijo/a que cierre los ojos y quite 2 de las medias. Pídale a su hijo/a que mire nuevamente y diga cuántas medias usted sacó y cuántas medias quedan.

Tercer paso Repita los pasos 1 y 2 con números diferentes, hasta que su hijo/a haga la actividad con confianza. Luego cambien los roles, de manera que usted deba contar y su hijo/a deba quitar las medias.

Dilo de varias maneras

Materiales frijoles, semillas de maíz, u otros objetos pequeños contables; papel, lápiz

Primer paso En un pedazo de papel, dibuje problemas de resta en blanco, como el siguiente: _____ $-$ _____ $=$ _____

Segundo paso Pídale a su hijo/a que coloque 5 frijoles sobre la mesa y que luego separe 3 frijoles del grupo. Pídale a su hijo/a que escriba el problema de resta, y que luego explique el problema de tres maneras diferentes: "Si comienzas con 5 y quitas 3, te quedan 2", "5 es 3 más que 2"; y "5 menos 3 es igual a 2". Repita la actividad usando números diferentes.

Name_____

Using the Minus Sign

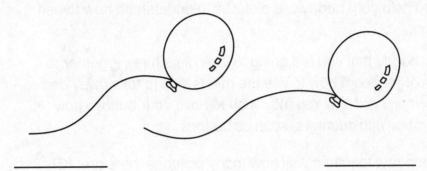

_____   .... _____

_____

_____   .... _____

_____

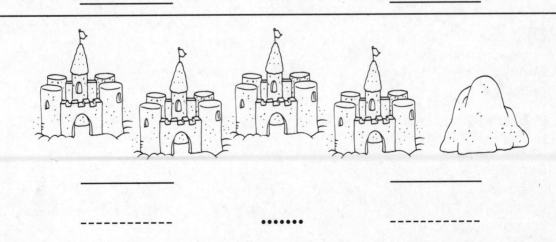

_____   .... _____

_____

Name_____

STUDY BUDDIES 21 COACH'S NOTES

Using the Minus Sign

Your goal: to help your buddy use pictures to understand how to use the minus sign.

1. Tell your buddy that you are going to look at pictures together to help him or her learn how to use the minus sign to take away and find how many are left. You may wish to have your buddy show each number with counters, such as buttons.

2. Look at top row together. Ask how many balloons there are. (2) How many are floating away? (2) Have your buddy write each number. Ask how many balloons are left. (0)

3. Look at the second row. Ask how many whole apples there were at the start. (4) How many apples were eaten? (1) Have your buddy write each number. Ask how many whole apples are left. (3)

4. Move to the last row. Ask how many sandcastles there were at the start. (5) How many sandcastles have been destroyed by the waves? (1) Have your buddy write each number. Ask how many sandcastles are left. (4)

Try this: Ask your buddy what happens if you count apples and sandcastles. How many apples and sandcastles were there at the start? (9) How many were taken away? (2) How many apples and sandcastles are left? (7)

STUDY BUDDIES 22 STUDENT PAGE

Finding the Difference

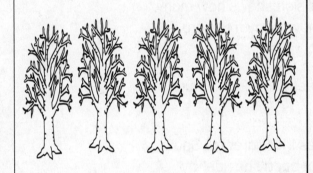

$$4 - 1 = 3$$

$$5 - 3 = \underline{}$$

$$6 - \underline{} = \underline{}$$

$$3 - \underline{} = \underline{}$$

STUDY BUDDIES 22 COACH'S NOTES

Finding the Difference

Your goal: to help your buddy identify the equal sign and practice subtracting numbers up to 6.

Tell your buddy that the pictures on the page show trees that a boy or girl saw during a long journey.

1. Ask your buddy how many leafy trees there are. (4) Show your buddy the 4 in the problem on the right. Tell your buddy that 1 tree was chopped down. Ask him or her to put an X on the tree that was chopped down. Remind your buddy that minus means something was taken away. Have your buddy point to the equal sign. Say that the number after the equal sign shows how many are left after some are taken away. Ask how many trees are left. (3) Read the whole statement aloud.

2. Repeat this procedure with the 5 bare trees. This time, your buddy will write the answer. (2)

3. For the next row, ask how many pine trees there are. (6) Show your buddy the 6 in the problem. Let your buddy decide, by making Xs, how many trees were chopped down. Write the number in the problem. How many trees are left? Write the number, and read the statement aloud with your buddy.

4. Do the same with the final row. Ask your buddy to cross out some of the palm trees and read the problem aloud as you write the numbers.

Try this: Help your buddy create new story problems to practice subtracting.

Name_____

FAMILY LETTER

CHAPTER 12

Counting and Number Patterns to 100

Dear Family,

Your child is learning about numbers up to 100, including how to recognize and write them, and how to order them in a "hundred chart" to explore patterns, such as *10 more* and *10 less*. He or she is also learning to skip count up to 100—that is, to count by 2s, 5s, and 10s.

You can help develop your child's skill at working with numbers up to 100 by doing the following activities together.

_____

Fill In the Blanks

Materials graph paper or plain paper; pencil

Step 1 On the paper, outline a 10-by-10 grid of squares.

Step 2 Fill in the numbers 1 through 10 left to right across the top and 1, 11, 21, ..., 91 down the left side. Fill in a few other randomly selected numbers.

Step 3 Ask your child to name a number at random. Using the numbers already filled in for reference, have the child write the new number in its proper location. Be sure to check that the number is placed correctly.

Step 4 Continue until your child can place any number quickly, correctly, and confidently.

Piks Counting

Step 1 Ask your child to count up to 100 by 2s, then by 5s, then by 10s.

Step 2 Once your child can do this confidently, ask the child to count backward from 100, by 2s: 100, 98, 96, ... Then have the child count backward by 5s, and then 10s. This is harder, so encourage your child to relax, not hurry, and not get frustrated over mistakes.

Step 3 Your child may want to try forward/backward skip counting by other numbers: by 3s, by 4s, and by 6s. Or your child may want to challenge you to try it!

1 2 3 CARTA A LA FAMILIA

Contar hasta 100 y patrones de números hasta 100

Estimada familia:

Su hijo/a aprenderá acerca de los números hasta el 100, incluyendo cómo reconocerlos y escribirlos, y cómo ordenarlos en una "tabla de centena" para descubrir patrones, como 10 más y 10 menos. También aprenderá a contar salteado hasta el 100, es decir, a contar de 2 en 2, de 5 en 5 y de 10 en 10.

Usted puede ayudar a su hijo/a a desarrollar las habilidades con números hasta el 100 haciendo juntos las actividades que se describen a continuación.

Completar los espacios

Materiales papel cuadriculado o en blanco; lápiz

Primer paso Dibuje una cuadrícula de 10 por 10 en el papel.

Segundo paso Escriba los números del 1 al 10 de izquierda a derecha en la fila superior y los números 1, 11, 21, ..., 91 en sentido vertical del lado izquierdo. Complete también algunos números más en distintos lugares de la cuadrícula.

Tercer paso Pídale a su hijo/a que nombre un número cualquiera. Usando los números ya escritos como referencia, pídale a su hijo/a que escriba el nuevo número en el lugar correcto. Verifique que el número esté en el lugar correcto en la tabla.

Cuarto paso Continúe hasta que su hijo/a pueda ubicar cualquier número en forma rápida y correcta y con confianza.

Contar salteado hacia adelante y hacia atrás

Primer paso Pídale a su hijo/a que cuente hasta 100 de 2 en 2, de 5 en 5, y luego de 10 en 10.

Segundo paso Una vez que su hijo/a haga esto con confianza, pídale que cuente hacia atrás de 2 en 2 comenzando en 100: 100, 98, 96, ... Luego pídale que cuente hacia atrás de 5 en 5 y de 10 en 10. Esto es más difícil; por eso, usted debe decirle a su hijo/a que lo haga con calma, sin apuro y que no se preocupe por los errores.

Tercer paso Quizá su hijo/a quiera probar a contar salteado hacia adelante y hacia atrás usando otros números: de 3 en 3, de 4 en 4 y de 6 en 6. ¡O quizá su hijo/a quiera desafiarle a usted a que intente hacerlo!

STUDY BUDDIES 23 STUDENT PAGE

Counting Groups of 10

Name_____

STUDY BUDDIES 23 COACH'S NOTES

Counting Groups of 10

Your goal: to help your buddy learn how to count large numbers of objects counting by 10s.

1. Tell your buddy to use skip counting by 10s for big groups of objects.

2. Have your buddy look at the first box and count the rockets in the first row. (10) How many rockets are there in both rows together? Lining the rockets up makes it easy to see that there are 10 rockets in each row. Counting by 10s is a quick way to count all the rockets. (20)

3. For the second box, ask how many planets there are in each row. (10) Have your buddy count by tens to find how many planets there are. (60)

4. For the third box, ask your buddy how many clouds there are. Have your buddy count by tens to find the total number of objects in the group. Have your buddy count aloud: "10, 20."

5. Your buddy should count, "10, 20, 30, 40" and say that there are 40 airplanes.

6. Have your buddy use the same method for the fifth and sixth boxes. How many moons are in the fifth box? (50) How many suns are in the sixth box? (60)

Try this: Gather 100 pennies or straws. Have your buddy group the objects by tens and count them to find the total.

Name_____

STUDY BUDDIES 24 STUDENT PAGE

Counting by 2s, 5s, and 10s

____

_____

There are ____ shoes.

_____

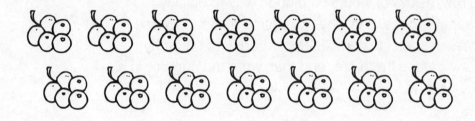

____

_____

There are ____ grapes.

_____

____

_____

There are ____ people in the buildings.

Name_____

STUDY BUDDIES 24 COACH'S NOTES

Counting by 2s, 5s, and 10s

Your goal: to help your buddy learn how to count large numbers of objects by counting by 2s, 5s, or 10s.

1. Tell your buddy that you are going to count by 2s, 5s, and 10s to count large groups of objects.

2. For the top row, ask your buddy what would be a good way to quickly count the total number of shoes, and why. (Counting by 2s, because there are 2 shoes per pair.) Invite your buddy to count by 2s, say how many shoes there are, and then write the number in the blank. (12)

3. For the second row, ask what would be a good way to quickly count the number of grapes, and why. (Counting by 5s, because there are 5 grapes in each cluster.) Ask your buddy to count by 5s, say how many grapes there are, and then write the number in the blank. (70)

4. For the last row, tell your buddy that even though he or she can't see them, there are exactly 10 people in each building. Ask what would be a good way to quickly count the total number of people in all the buildings, and why. (Counting by 10s, because there are 10 people per building.) Have your buddy count by 10s, say how many people there are altogether, and then write the number in the blank. (40)

Try this: Have your buddy count the same group of 50 objects, first by 2s, then by 5s, and lastly by 10s.